Time to Go

Read the words. Write them in the boxes.

dad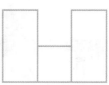

hat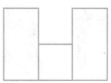

coat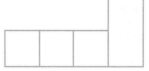

Practice reading these words.

time   put   go   my   it   on   to

I get my coat.
I put it on.

Level A

I get my hat.
I put it on.

I get my dad.
Time to go.

Remembering the Story

Draw a line to show what happened.

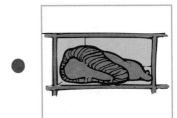

Seeing Words

Circle the words that are the same as the first word in each row.

coat	(coat)	time	(coat)
hat	home	hat	hat
dad	dad	dad	put
this	time	this	this
it	it	is	it

Hang Them Up

Cut out the coat and hat. Glue them onto the correct hook.

Hang up the coat.

glue

Hang up the hat.

glue

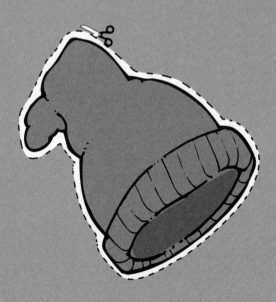

Read and Think

Read each sentence. Circle the correct item.

This is a red hat.

This is a blue coat.

This is my dad.

Same Sound

Circle **yes** if the picture begins with the same sound as **dad**.

Pictures: dog, coat, doll, door, hat, duck, dinosaur, bike

Level A

The
Pet Store

Read the words. Write them in the boxes.

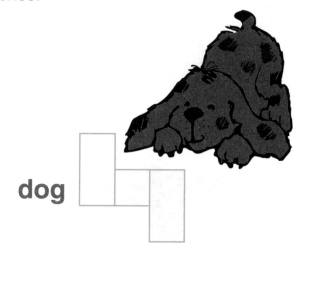

dog

cat

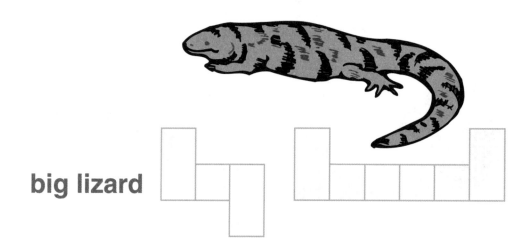

big lizard

Practice reading these words.

I   see   Hi   Good-bye   the

I go to the pet store.
I see a dog.
Hi, dog.

I go to the pet store.
I see a cat.
Hi, cat.

Level A

I go to the pet store.
I see a big lizard.
Good-bye, big lizard!

Remembering the Story

Circle the picture(s) to answer each question.

Which animals did the girl see?

cat   dog   lizard

Which animals did the girl like?

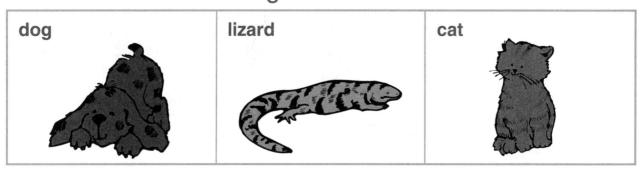

dog   lizard   cat

Which animal scared the girl?

lizard   dog   cat

Which animal would you like to buy?

cat   lizard   dog

Where Do the Animals Belong?

Cut and glue to show where each animal belongs.

glue

glue

This is a lizard.

glue

This is a dog.

This is a cat.

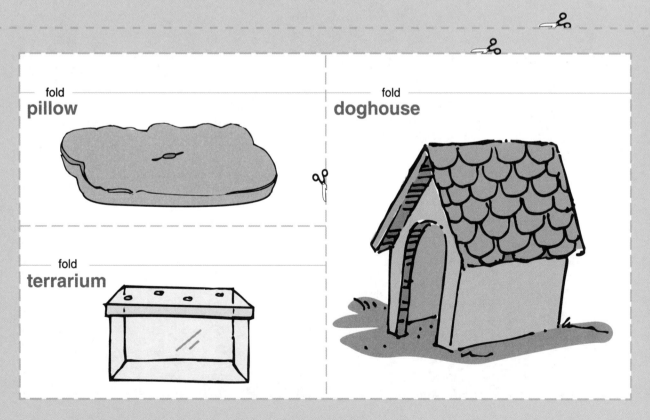

fold
pillow

fold
doghouse

fold
terrarium

Level A

Trace and Match

Trace the words. Draw lines to match.

Good-bye •

•

Hi •

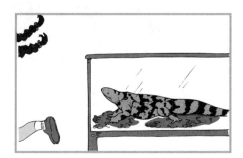

•

Same Sound

Cut and glue to show which pictures begin with the same sound as **cat**.

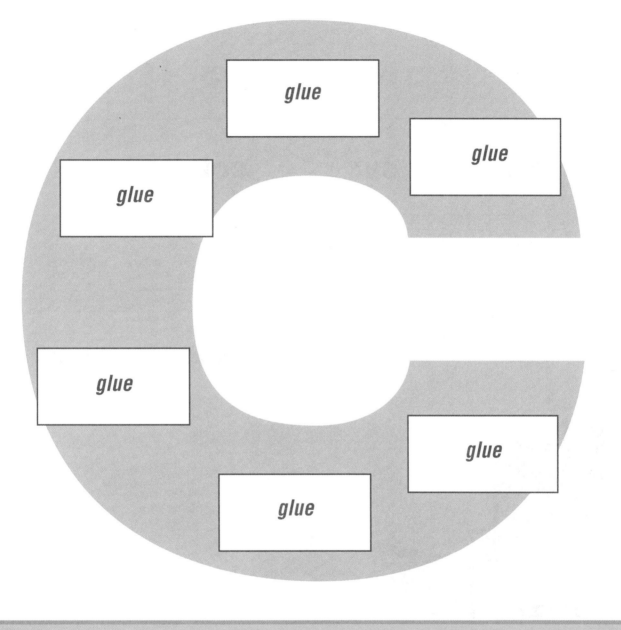

glue

glue

glue

glue

glue

glue

Pictures: car, bird, caterpillar, comb, corn, carrot, dog, can

Seeing Words

Circle the words that are the same as the first word in each row.

pet	pat	(pet)	(pet)
cat	cat	cot	cat
dog	dog	dog	dig
see	see	store	see

A Pair

Read the words. Write them in the boxes.

1

one

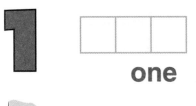
foot

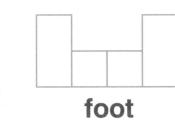
sock

shoe

2

two

feet

socks

shoes

Practice reading these words.

I   see

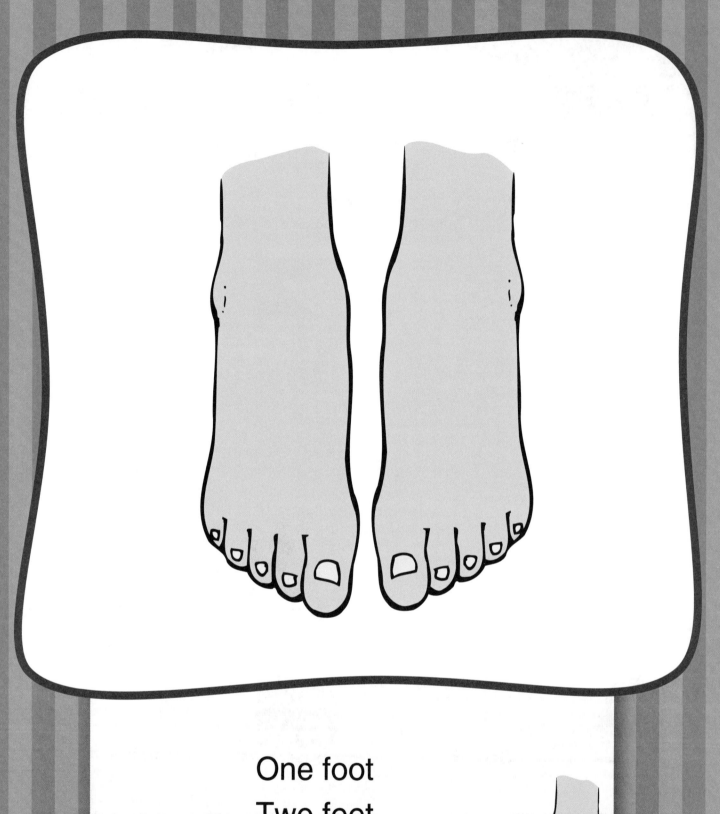

One foot
Two feet
I see two feet.

One sock
Two socks
I see two socks.

One shoe
Two shoes
I see two shoes.

Remembering the Story

Cut and glue the socks and shoes onto the feet.

Seeing Words

Circle the words that are the same as the first word in each row.

one	on	(one)	(one)
two	to	two	two
feet	feet	foot	feet
see	see	see	we

How Many?

Circle the number word to show how many.

(one)

two

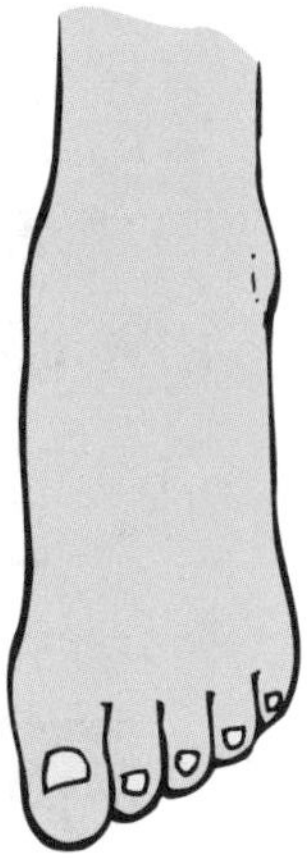

one

two

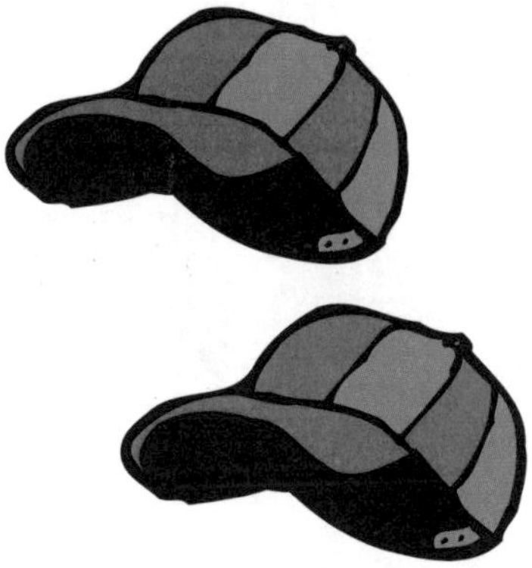

one

two

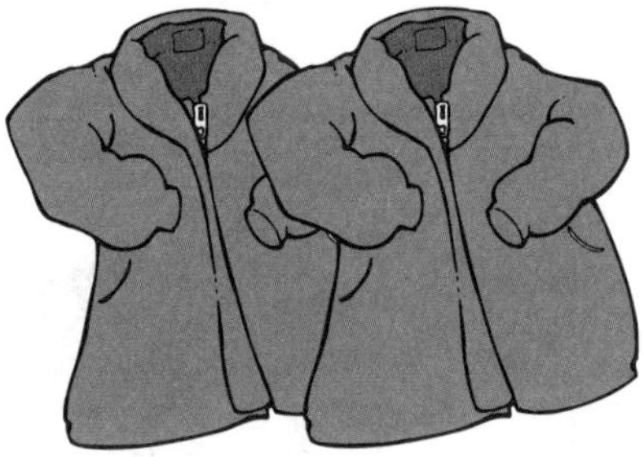

one

two

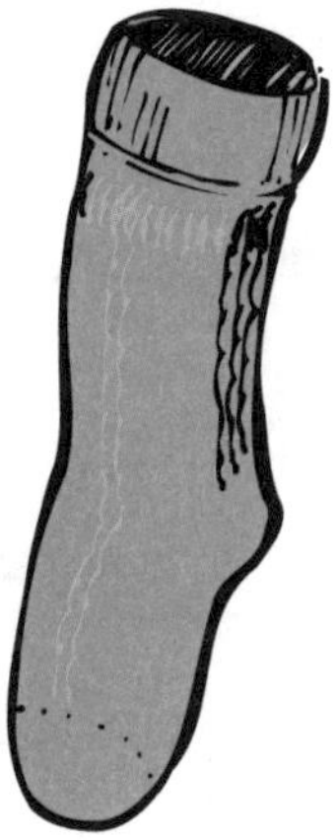

one

two

one

two

Same Sound

Circle the pictures that begin with the same sound as **sock**.

How many began with the same sound?

Pictures: seal, cup, sand, seven, sun, saddle, dog, mouse

Whose Shoes?

Draw a line to show to whom each shoe belongs.

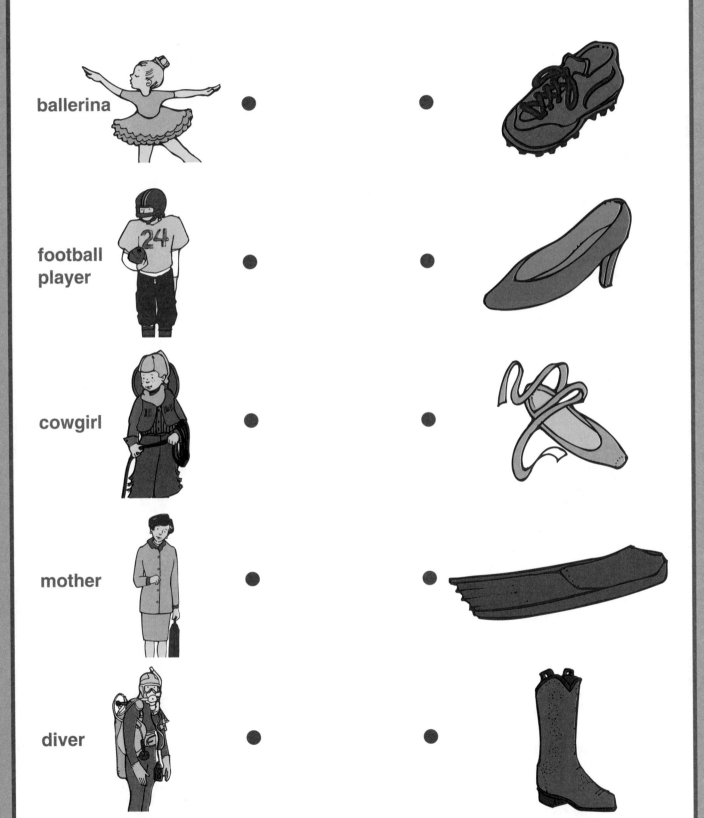

ballerina

football player

cowgirl

mother

diver

4

Up and Down

Read the words. Write them in the boxes.

up

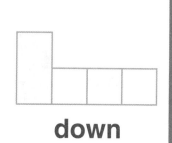

down

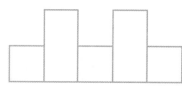

slide

we

Practice reading these words.

are   **on**   **ground**

Level A

We are up.

We are up on the slide.

We go down.

We go down the slide.

We are down.
We are on the ground.

Remembering the Story

Read each sentence. Mark the box that shows what each sentence means.

We go up.

We go down.

We are on the ground.

Cut and Glue Fun

Cut and glue each picture under the correct word.

up	down	up	down
glue	*glue*	*glue*	*glue*

flag   ladder

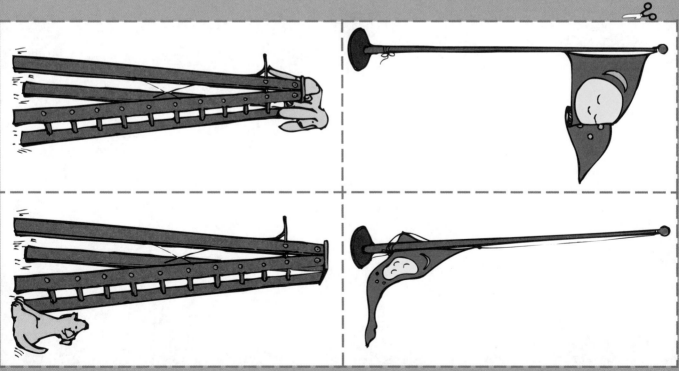

On the Playground

Draw to show yourself on the playground.

I am up.

I am down.

Up or Down?

Look at each picture. Circle **up** or **down**.

up   down

up   down

up   down

up   down

5

Where Does It Sleep?

Read the words. Write them in the boxes.

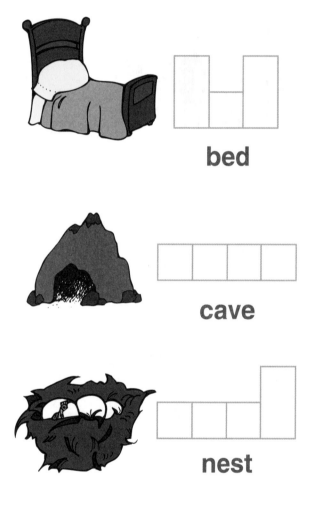

bed

cave

nest

boy

bear

bird

Practice reading these words.

in   a   sleeps   see

See the bird.

The bird sleeps in a nest.

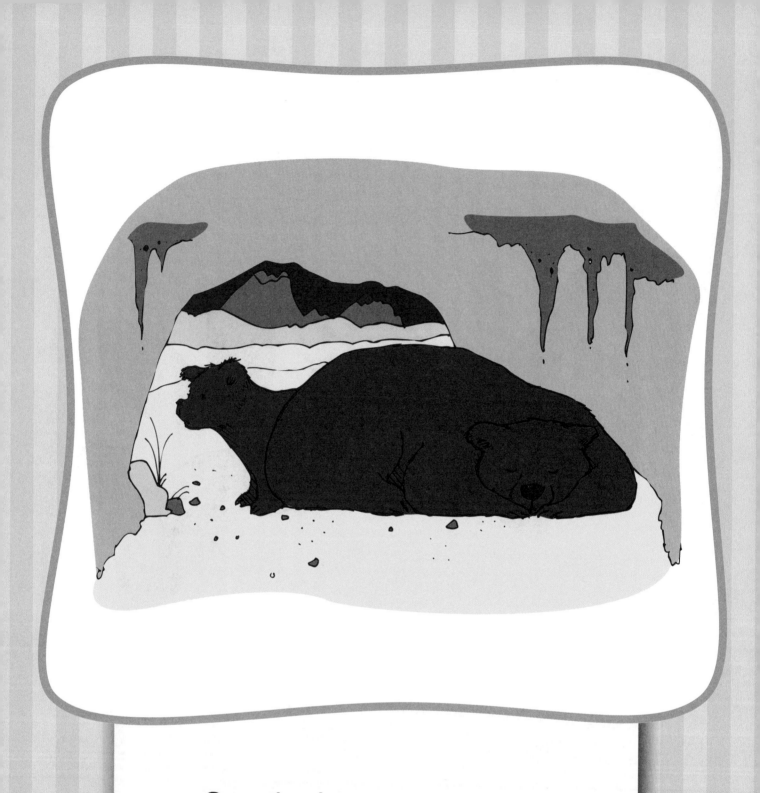

See the bear.

The bear sleeps in a cave.

See the boy.

The boy sleeps in a bed.

Remembering the Story

Draw a line to show where each person or animal sleeps.

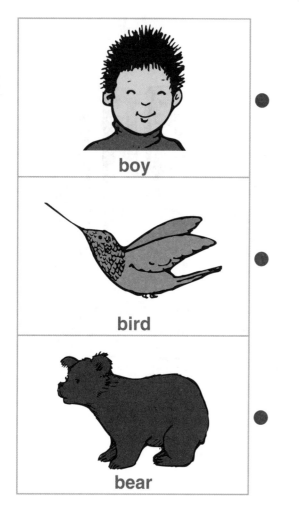

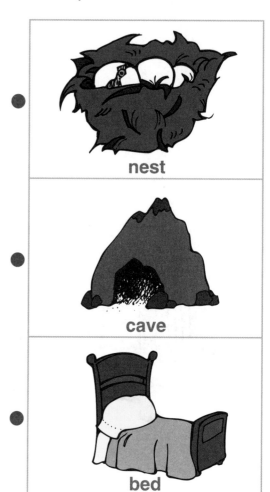

Draw a picture that shows where you sleep.

Are You Awake?

Look at each picture. Cut and glue each picture under **Awake** or **Asleep**.

Awake		Asleep	
glue	glue	glue	glue
glue	glue	glue	glue

Skill: Vocabulary Development

Find the Word

Write the correct word to complete each sentence.

I see a _____.
boy   nest

I see a _____.
cave   bear

I see a _____.
bird   bed

Same Sound

Circle the pictures that begin with the same sound as **boy**.

Pictures: bear, balloon, cat, bed, bus, nest, book, bird, cave, ball, bike, bat

Level A

6

We Go for a Ride

Read the words. Write them in the boxes.

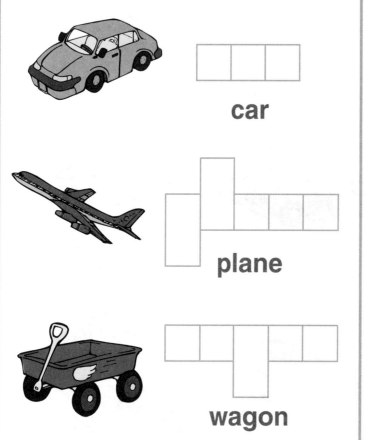

car

plane

wagon

yes

no

we

Practice reading these words.

in   ride   go   for

We go for a ride.

In a wagon? Yes.

We go for a ride in a wagon.

We go for a ride.

In a wagon? No.

In a car? Yes.

We go for a ride in a car.

We go for a ride.

In a wagon? No.

In a car? No.

In a plane? Yes.

We go for a ride in a plane.

Remembering the Story

Circle the correct picture(s) to answer the questions.

Who was in the wagon?

girl   doll   bear   dad

Who was in the car?

girl   doll   bear   dad

Who was in the plane?

girl   doll   bear   dad

Would you ride in a wagon?    yes    no

Same Sound

Cut and glue to show which pictures begin with the same sound as **wagon**.

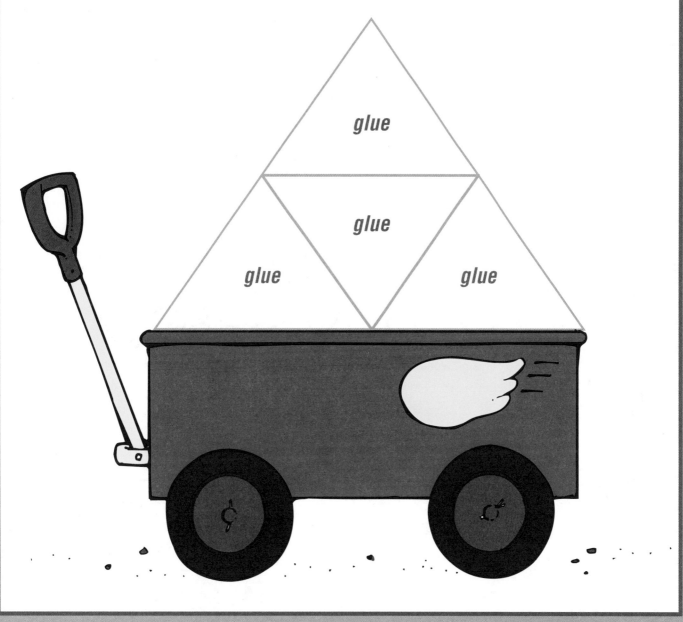

Pictures: worm, rattle, wolf, wand, walrus

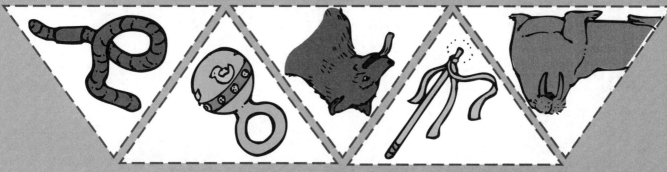

Level A

Reading Colors

Color the car **red**.

Color the wagon **blue**.

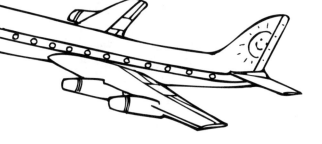

Color the plane **green**.

I Can Ride

Can you ride in or on it? Look at each picture. Circle **yes** or **no**.

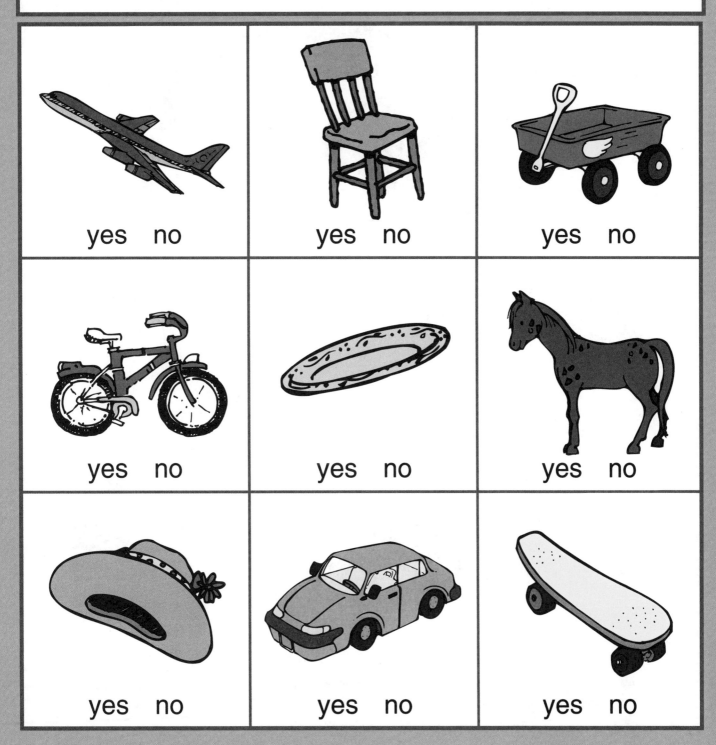

yes   no

yes   no

yes   no

yes   no

yes   no

yes   no

yes   no

yes   no

yes   no

Pictures: plane, chair, wagon, bike, dish, horse, hat, car, skateboard

Level A

7

Big and Little

Read the words. Write them in the boxes.

big car

little car

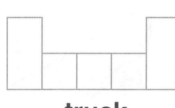

truck

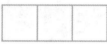

1

one

2

two

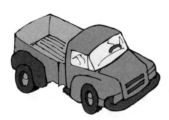

3

three

Practice reading these words.

stop   **and**   **go**

One big car

Two big cars

Two big cars stop and go.

One, two, three
Three little cars
Three little cars stop and go.

See the big truck.

Two big cars go on the truck.

Three little cars go on the truck.

The big truck can stop and go.

Match It Up

Read the words. Draw a line to show what they mean.

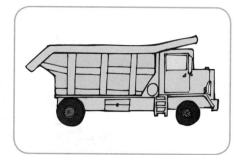

big car ●   ●

big truck ●   ●

little car ●   ●

Draw a big truck and a little truck.

Level A

Same Sound

Cut and glue to show which pictures begin with the same sound as **lion**.

glue

glue

glue

glue	glue	glue

Pictures: rhino, leaf, table, lamp, llama, lock, lunchbox, log

57

Level A

How Many?

Trace the number words. Draw a line to match each number word to a picture.

three •

one •

four •

two •

•

•

•

•

8

Which Hat?

Read the words. Write them in the boxes.

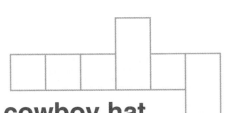 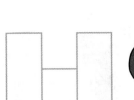 

cowboy hat

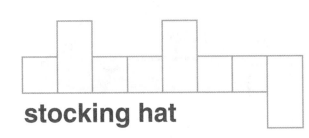 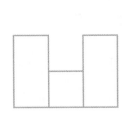 

stocking hat

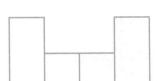 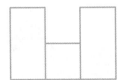 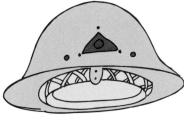

hard hat

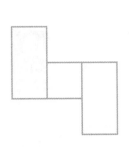 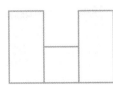 

top hat

Practice reading these words.

will   it   which   wants   choose   be

Which hat will you choose?
Will it be a cowboy hat?
Will it be a hard hat?

Which hat will you choose?
Will it be a stocking hat?
Will it be a top hat?

Alice wants a cowboy hat.

Yongjun wants a hard hat.

Minseo wants a stocking hat.

Arthur wants a top hat.

Which hat do you want?

Remembering the Story

Circle the hats from the story.

cowboy hat

football helmet

top hat

stocking hat

party hat

hard hat

beret

ball cap

Write the name of each hat.

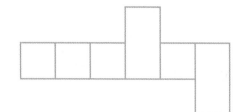

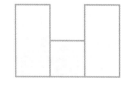

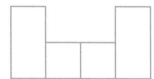

Whose Hat?

Draw a line to show to whom each hat belongs.

**football
player**

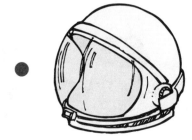

astronaut

doctor

clown

Level A

It Rhymes with Hat

Cut and glue to show which pictures rhyme with **hat**.

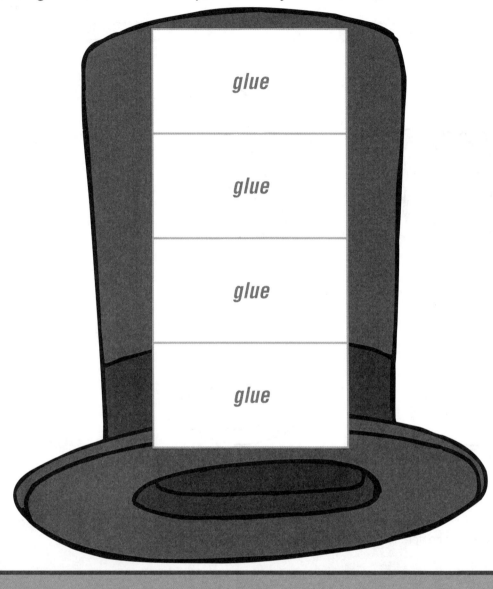

Pictures: car, cat, bat, dog, bat, mat

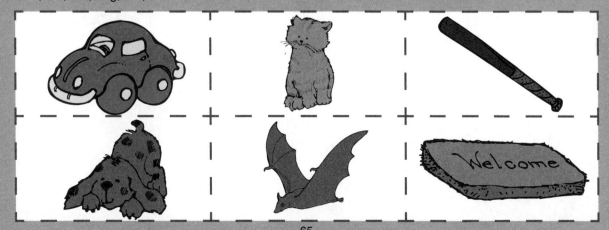

65

Level A

Same Sound

Circle the pictures that begin with the same sound as **hat**.

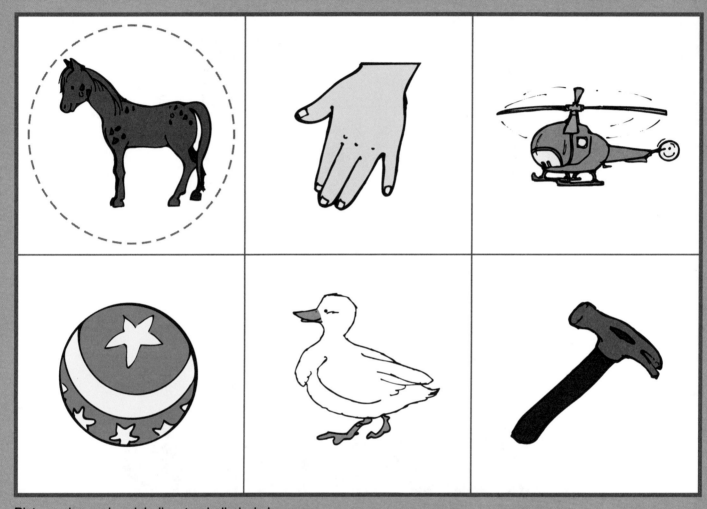

Pictures: horse, hand, helicopter, ball, duck, hammer

Level A

9

In the Sky

Read the words. Write them in the boxes.

plane

sun

cloud

kite

rain

Practice reading these words.

see　　**do**　　**flies**　　**fell**　　**by**　　**is**

Do you see the sun?

Do you see the plane?

The plane is in the sky.

The sun is in the sky, too.

Do you see the clouds?
Do you see the kite?
The kite flies up by the clouds.

Do you see the clouds?
Do you see the rain?
Do you see the kite?
The kite fell down.

Remembering the Story

Show the order of the story. Draw a line from each picture to the correct number.

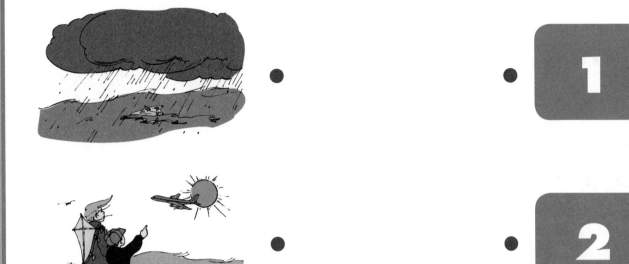
•

• **1**

•

• **2**

•

• **3**

Draw a picture of a kite.

Seeing Words

Circle the word that is the same as the first word in each row.

rain	rain	train	run
sun	sun	son	suns
plane	plan	plane	plain
kite	kits	kit	kite
look	lock	lick	look

Level A

Same Sound

Cut and glue to show which pictures begin with the same sound as **rain**.

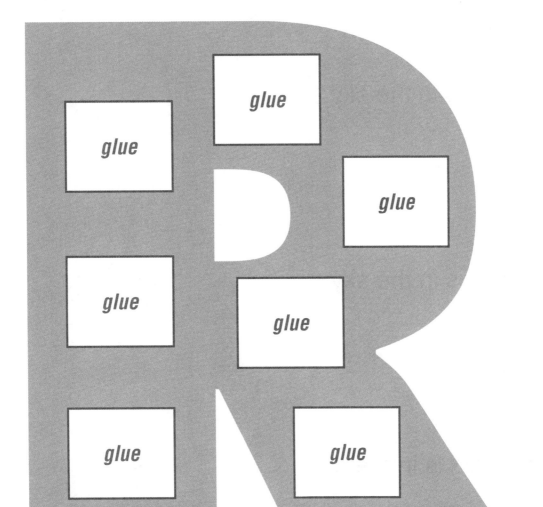

Pictures: rabbit, raccoon, plane, rake, radio, car, rock, tent, refrigerator, rooster

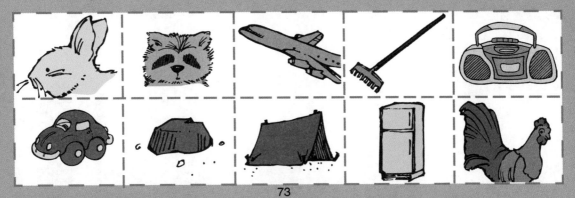

Level A

What's in the Sky?

Read each sentence. Draw a line to the correct picture.

The **kite** is in the sky.

The **sun** is in the sky.

The **cloud** is in the sky.

10

Little Quackers

Read the words. Write them in the boxes.

quiet

duck

quack

book

Practice reading these words.

look   not   this   spot

This is a quiet spot.
I will look at a book.

Look! A duck.

I see a duck.

Quack!

Quack, quack, quack,
quack, quack, quack!

This is not a quiet spot.
I will go.

Remembering the Story

Show the order of the story. Write **1**, **2**, or **3** in each box.

Quack, Quack, Quack, Quack!

This is a quiet spot.

Quack!

Noisy Animals

Draw a line to show which animal makes each sound.

cow

●   ● **Peep**

dog

●   ● **Quack**

chick

●   ● **Moo**

cat

●   ● **Woof-Woof**

duck

●   ● **Meow**

Level A

The Sound of *qu*

Cut and glue the pictures that begin with the sound of **qu** onto the **quilt**.

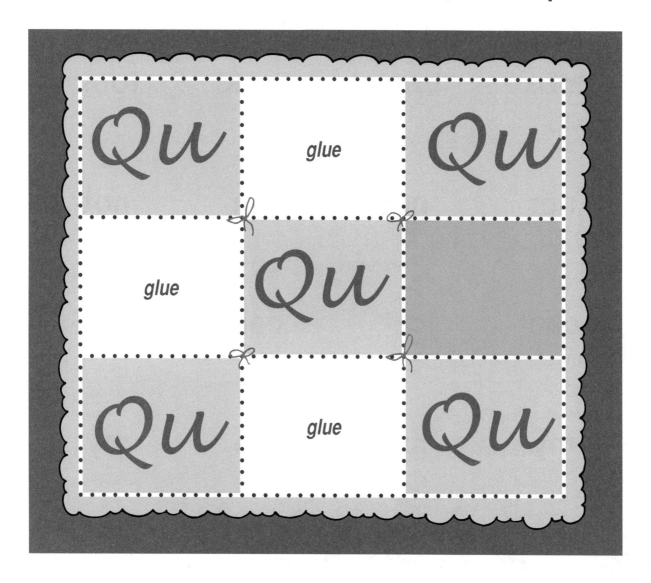

Pictures: queen, quilt, question mark, car

Level A

Seeing Words

Circle the words that are the same as the first word in each row.

look	book	look	look
not	not	ton	not
can	cat	can	can
my	my	me	my

11

Herbie

Read the words. Write them in the boxes.

Herbie

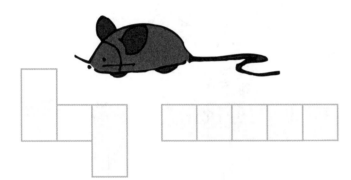

toy mouse

Practice reading these words.

jump   has   sleep   can   play

Level A

Herbie is a cat.
Herbie can jump.

Jump, Herbie, jump.
Meow!

Herbie can play.
He has a toy mouse.

Play, Herbie, play.
Meow!

Herbie can sleep.

He sleeps with the toy mouse.

Sleep, Herbie, sleep.

Purr!

Same Sound

Cut and glue to show which pictures begin with the same sound as **jump**.

glue   glue

glue

glue

glue   glue

✂

Pictures: juggler, jet, jar, cat, jacks, juice, wagon, jack-in-the-box

87   Level A

Seeing Words

Circle the words that are the same as the first word in each row.

jump	jump	run	jump
play	pig	play	play
sleep	sleep	slow	sleep
meow	meow	mom	meow
cat	car	cat	cat

Remembering the Story

Circle the correct picture to show each answer.

Herbie is a _____.

bird

cat

dog

Herbie likes to _____.

eat

run

play

Herbie has a _____.

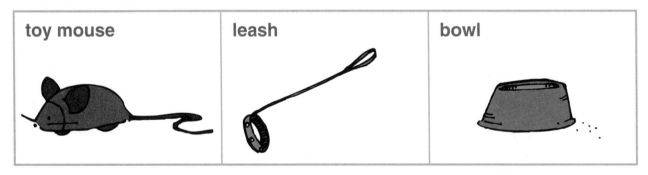

toy mouse

leash

bowl

At the end of the story, Herbie _____.

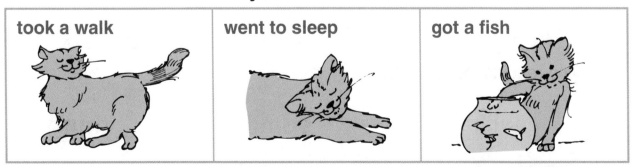

took a walk

went to sleep

got a fish

12

Will It Float?

Read the words. Write them in the boxes.

float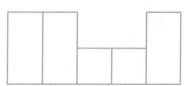

sink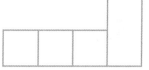

think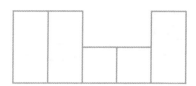

Practice reading these words.

I   will   it   something   things

Some things float.
Some things sink.

I think it will float.

Will it float?
Will it sink?

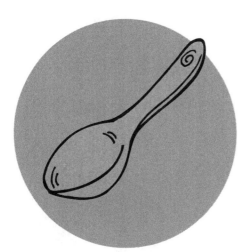

I think it will sink.

Will it float?
Will it sink?

Will it float?
Will it sink?

I think it will sink.

Will it float?
Will it sink?

I think it will float.

Some things float.

Some things sink.

Can you find something
that floats?

Will It Float?

Connect the dots in ABC order.

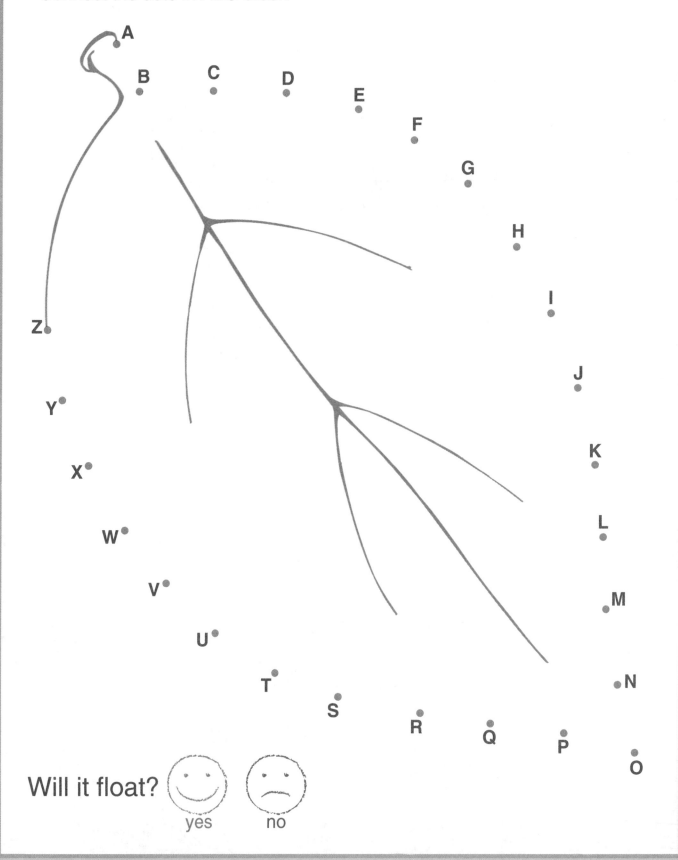

Will it float?   yes   no

It Rhymes

Cut and glue to show the pictures that rhyme with **float**.
Cut and glue to show the pictures that rhyme with **sink**.

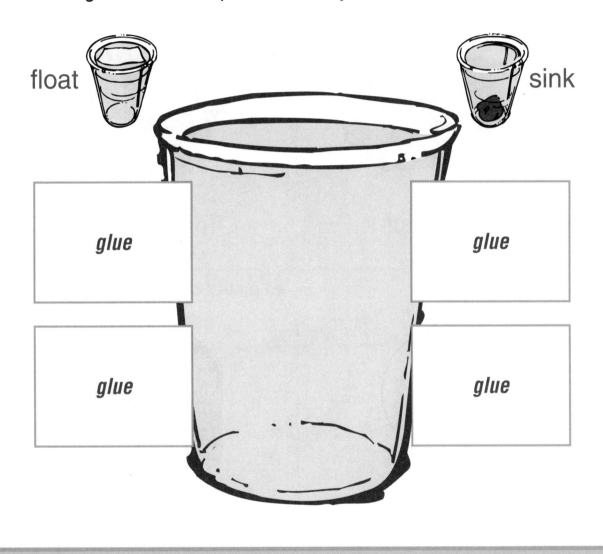

Pictures: coat, pink, boat, drink

Will It Float?

Circle **float** or **sink**.

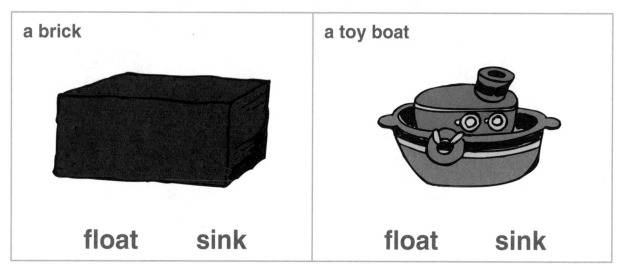

a brick

float   sink

a toy boat

float   sink

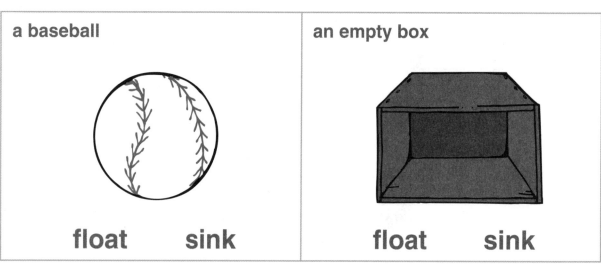

a baseball

float   sink

an empty box

float   sink